UKULELE
SIMPLE CHRISTMAS SONGS

ISBN 978-1-4950-9725-6

HAL•LEONARD®

7777 W. BLUEMOUND RD. P.O. BOX 13819 MILWAUKEE, WI 53213

Visit Hal Leonard Online at
www.halleonard.com

All I Want for Christmas Is You

Words and Music by Mariah Carey and Walter Afanasieff

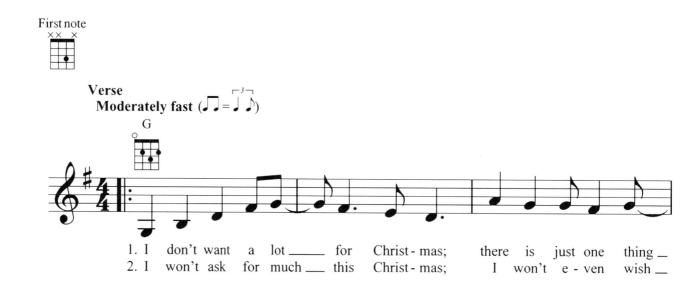

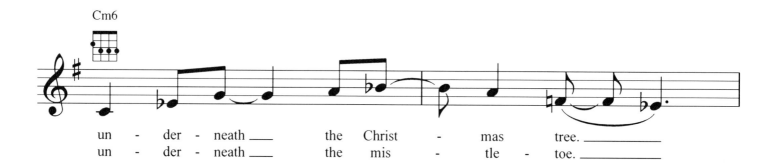

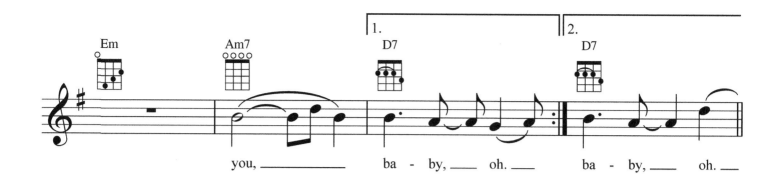

you, _____ ba - by, ___ oh. ___ ba - by, ___ oh. ___

Bridge

___ All the lights ___ are shin - ing so bright - ly ev - 'ry - where, ___

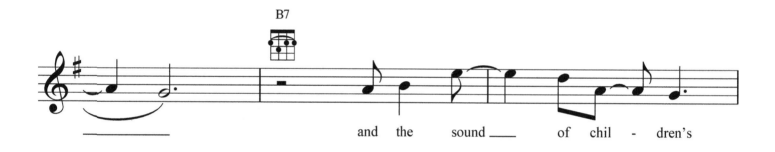

_____ and the sound ___ of chil - dren's

laugh - ter fills ___ the air. _____ And ev - 'ry - one __

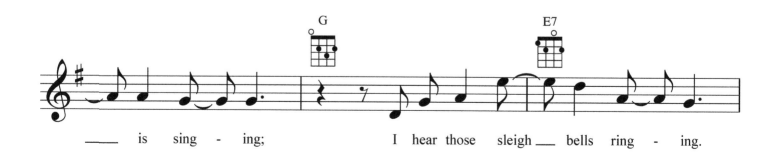

___ is sing - ing; I hear those sleigh ___ bells ring - ing.

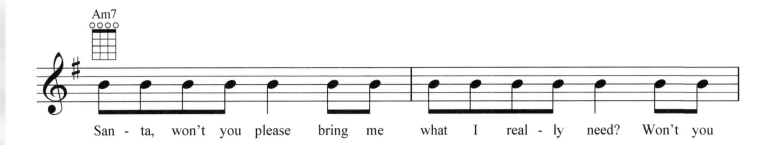

San - ta, won't you please bring me what I real - ly need? Won't you

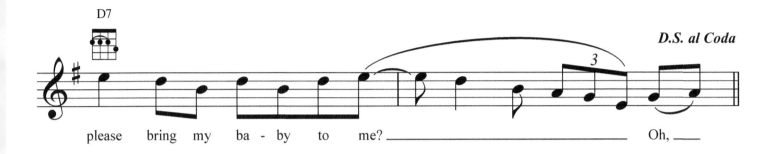

D.S. al Coda

please bring my ba - by to me? _____ Oh, ___

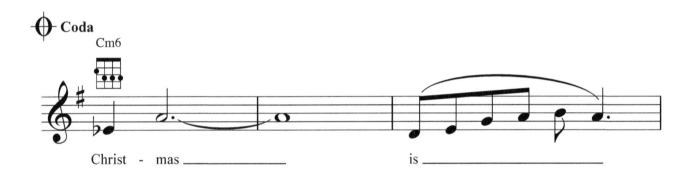

Coda

Christ - mas _____ is _____

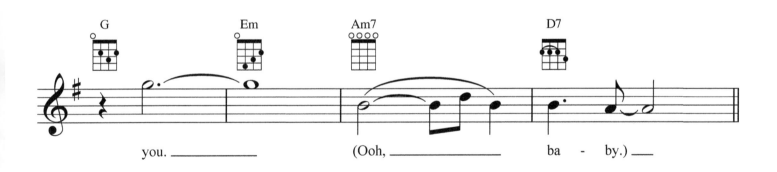

you. _____ (Ooh, _____ ba - by.) ___

Outro

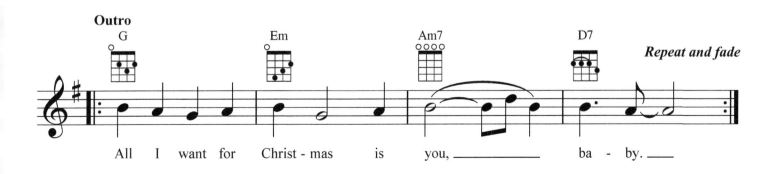

Repeat and fade

All I want for Christ - mas is you, _____ ba - by. ___

All I Want for Christmas Is My Two Front Teeth

Words and Music by Don Gardner

Ev - 'ry - bod - y stops and stares at me. _____

These two teeth are gone as you can see. _____

I don't know just who to blame for this ca - tas - tro - phe, but

my one wish on Christ - mas Eve is as plain as it can be!

Chorus

All I want for Christ-mas is my two front teeth, my two front teeth, see my two front teeth.

Baby, It's Cold Outside

from the Motion Picture NEPTUNE'S DAUGHTER
By Frank Loesser

Believe

from Warner Bros. Pictures' THE POLAR EXPRESS
Words and Music by Glen Ballard and Alan Silvestri

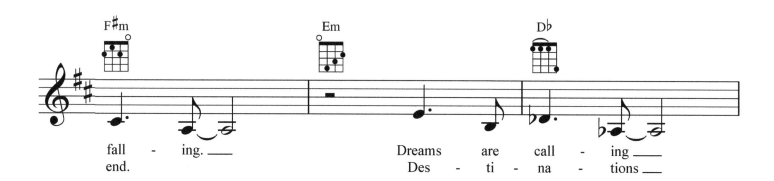

1. Chil - dren ___ sleep - ing, ___ snow is soft - ly
2. Trains move ___ quick - ly ___ to their jour - ney's

fall - ing. ___ Dreams are call - ing ___
end. Des - ti - na - tions ___

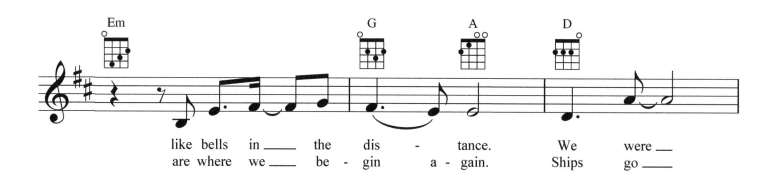

like bells in ___ the dis - tance. We were ___
are where we ___ be - gin a - gain. Ships go ___

dream - ers ___ not so long ___ a - go, ___
sail - ing ___ far a - cross the sea, ___

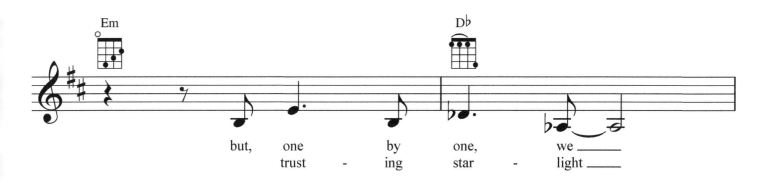

but,   one   by   one,   we _____
trust -   ing   star -   light _____

        all   had ____   to   grow _____   up.
to   get   where __   they   need   to   be.

Pre-Chorus

When   it   seems __   the   mag -   ic   slipped a - way,   we
When   it   seems __   that   we __ have   lost   our   way,   we

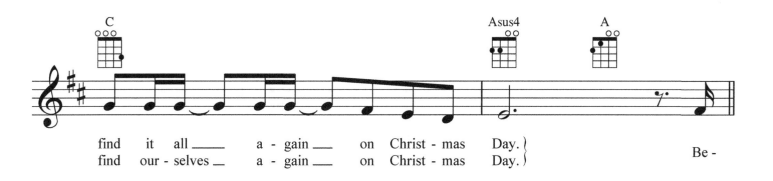

find   it   all ____   a - gain ___   on   Christ - mas   Day. }
find   our - selves __   a - gain ___   on   Christ - mas   Day. }

                                                                       Be -

Chorus

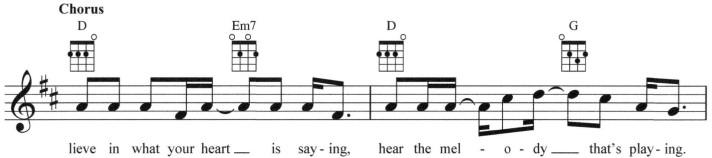

lieve   in   what   your   heart __   is   say - ing,   hear   the   mel -   o - dy ____   that's   play - ing.

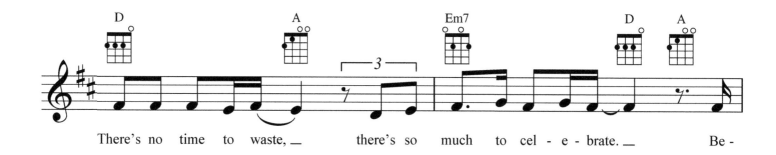

There's no time to waste, __ there's so much to cel - e - brate. __ Be -

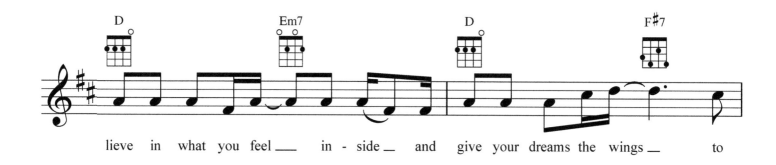

lieve in what you feel __ in - side __ and give your dreams the wings __ to

fly. You have ev - 'ry - thing you __ need __ if you just __

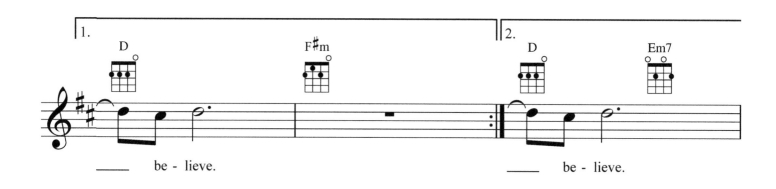

1. __ be - lieve.   2. __ be - lieve.

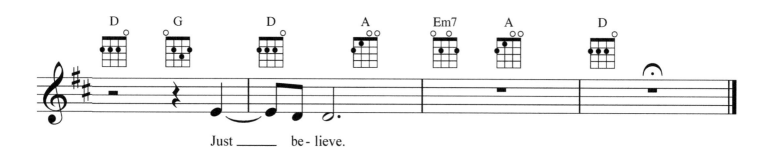

Just __ be - lieve.

Caroling, Caroling

Words by Wihla Hutson
Music by Alfred Burt

Blue Christmas

Words and Music by Billy Hayes and Jay Johnson

A Child Is Born

Music by Thad Jones
Lyrics by Alex Wilder

First note

Verse
Slow Jazz Ballad

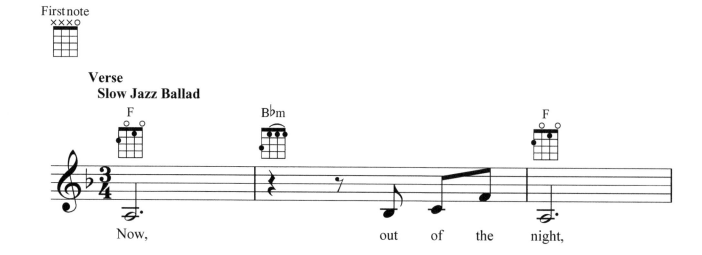

Now, out of the night,

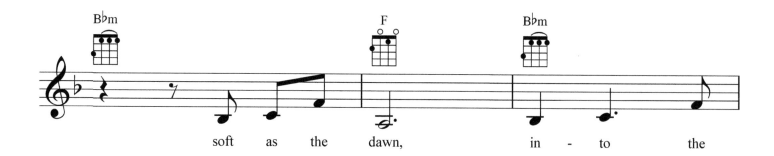

soft as the dawn, in - to the

light. This child,

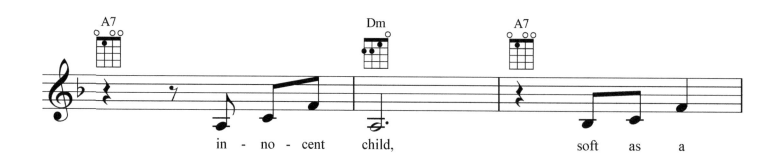

in - no - cent child, soft as a

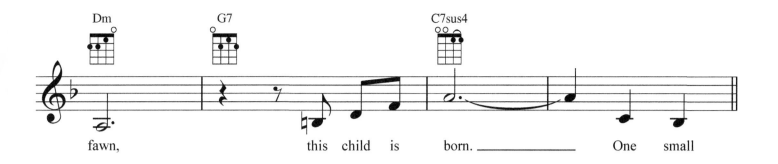

fawn, this child is born. _____ One small

Outro-Verse

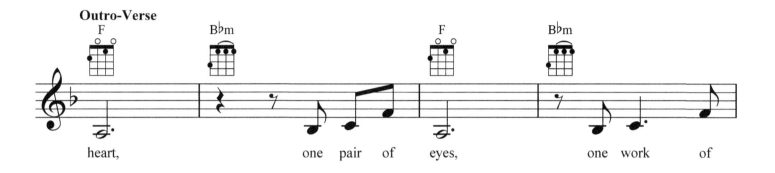

heart, one pair of eyes, one work of

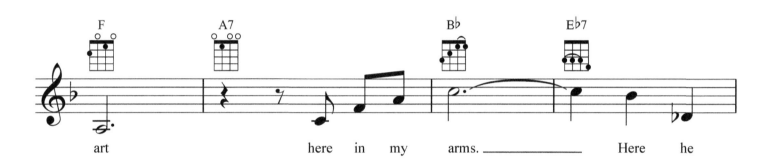

art here in my arms. _____ Here he

lies, trust - ing ____ and warm, blessed in ____ this

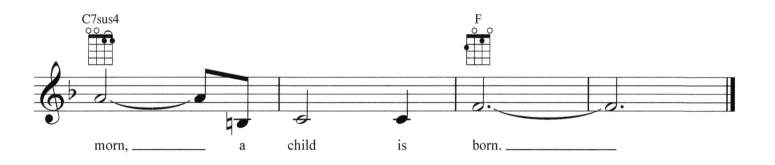

morn, _____ a child is born. _____

The Chipmunk Song

Words and Music by Ross Bagdasarian

Christmas Time Is Here

from A CHARLIE BROWN CHRISTMAS
Words by Lee Mendelson
Music by Vince Guaraldi

First note

Verse
Slowly

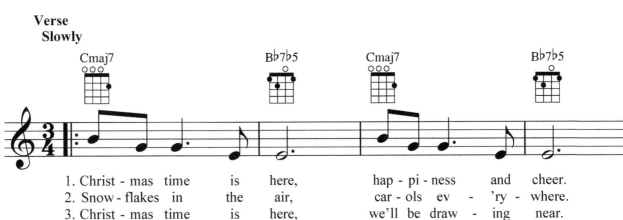

1. Christ - mas time   is   here,   hap - pi - ness   and   cheer.
2. Snow - flakes in   the   air,   car - ols ev - 'ry - where.
3. Christ - mas time   is   here,   we'll be draw - ing   near.

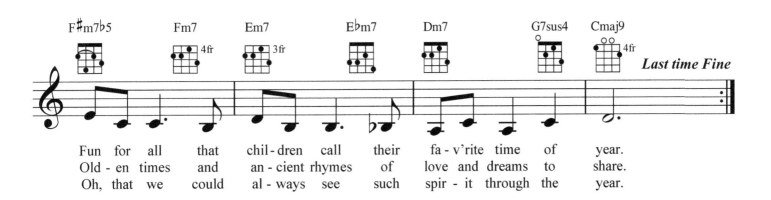

Fun for all   that   chil - dren call   their   fa - v'rite time   of   year.
Old - en times and   an - cient rhymes of   love and dreams to   share.
Oh, that we   could   al - ways see   such   spir - it through the   year.

Bridge

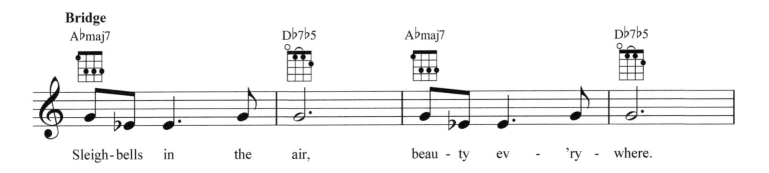

Sleigh - bells in   the   air,   beau - ty ev - 'ry - where.

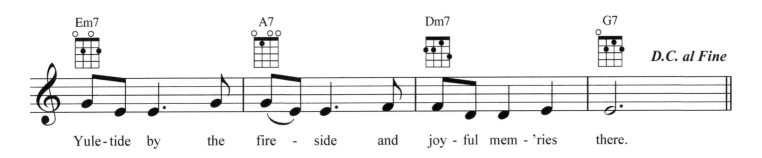

Yule - tide by   the   fire - side and   joy - ful mem - 'ries   there.

The Christmas Song
(Chestnuts Roasting on an Open Fire)

Music and Lyric by Mel Tormé and Robert Wells

Christmas Wrapping

Words and Music by Chris Butler

First note

Verse
Moderately fast

1. Bah, hum - bug! No, that's too strong. 'Cause it
2., 3. See additional lyrics

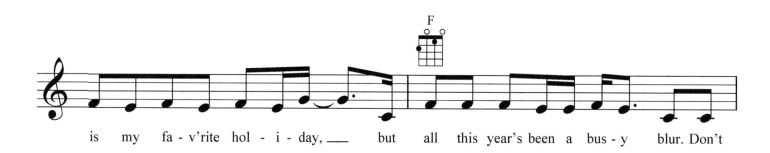

is my fa - v'rite hol - i - day, ___ but all this year's been a bus - y blur. Don't

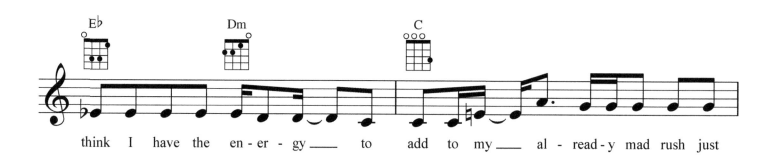

think I have the en - er - gy ___ to add to my ___ al - read - y mad rush just

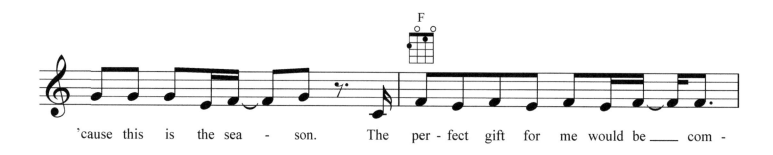

'cause this is the sea - son. The per - fect gift for me would be ___ com -

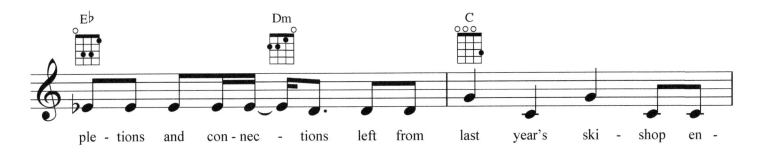

ple - tions and con - nec - tions left from last year's ski - shop en -

coun - ter, most in - t'rest - ing. ___ Had his num - ber but nev - er the time. ___

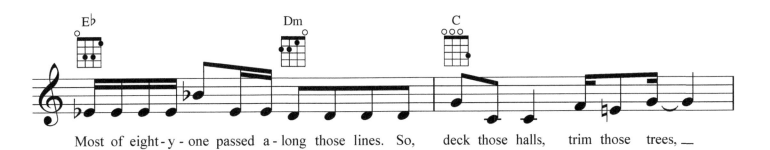

Most of eight - y - one passed a - long those lines. So, deck those halls, trim those trees, ___

raise up cups of Christ - mas cheer. ___ I just need to catch ___ my breath.

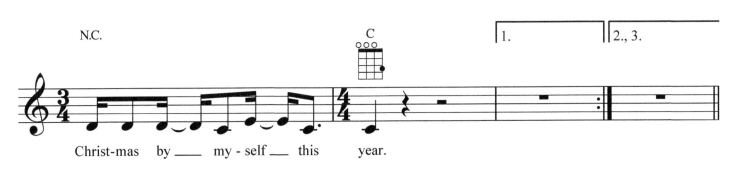

Christ - mas by ___ my - self ___ this year.

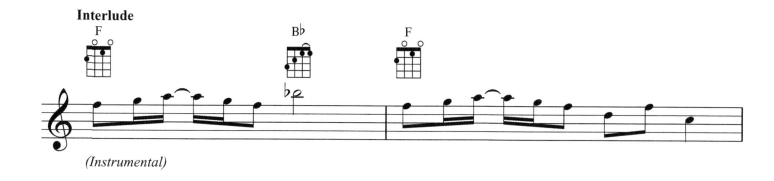

Interlude

(Instrumental)

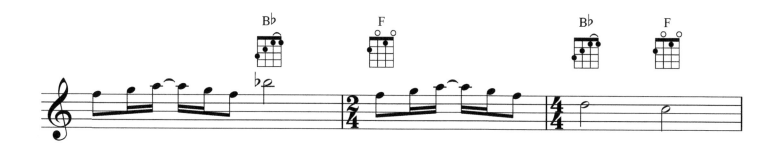

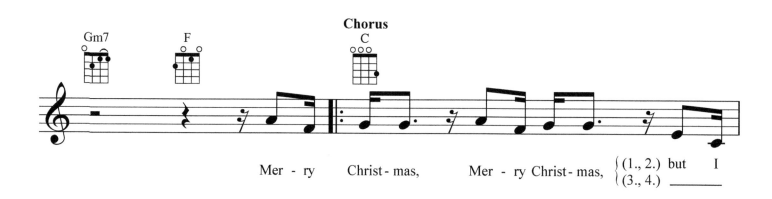

Chorus

Mer - ry Christ - mas, Mer - ry Christ - mas, { (1., 2.) but I { (3., 4.) ———

think I'll miss ___ this one ___ this year. ___ } Mer - ry
could - n't miss ___ this one ___ this year. ___ }

1., 3.

Christ - mas, Mer - ry Christ - mas, { but I { ———

think I'll miss ___ this one ___ this year. ___ } Mer - ry
could - n't miss ___ this one ___ this year. ___ }

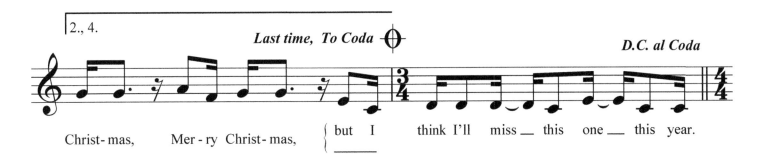

2., 4.   *Last time, To Coda* ⊕   *D.C. al Coda*

Christ- mas, Mer - ry Christ- mas, { but I think I'll miss __ this one __ this year.
___ }

⊕ **Coda**

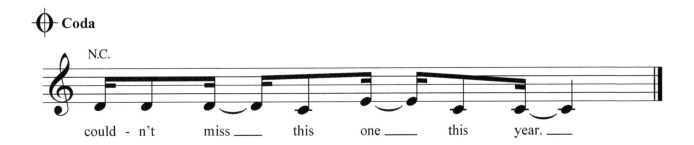

N.C.

could - n't miss ___ this one ___ this year. ___

Additional Lyrics

2. Calendar pictures, frozen landscape chilled this room for twenty-four days.
   Evergreens, sparkling snow; get this winter over with!
   Flashback to springtime, saw him again. Would've been good to go for lunch.
   Couldn't agree when we're both free. We tried; we said we'd keep in touch.
   Didn't, of course, till summertime. Out to the beach to his boat; could I join him?
   No, this time it was me; sunburn in the third degree.
   Now the calendar's just one page; of course, I am excited.
   Tonight's the night I set my mind not to do too much about it.

3. A&P has pride in me with the world's smallest turkey.
   Already in the oven, nice and hot. Oh, damn! Guess what I forgot?
   So, on with the boots, back out in the snow to the only all-night grocery,
   When what to my wondering eyes should appear? In the line is that guy
       I've been chasing all year!
   "I'm spending this one alone," he said. "Need a break; this year's been crazy."
   I said, "Me too, but why are you…? You mean, you forgot cranberries, too?"
   Then suddenly we laughed and laughed, caught on to what was happening:
   That Christmas magic's brought this tale to a very happy ending.

Do They Know It's Christmas?
(Feed the World)
Words and Music by Bob Geldof and Midge Ure

no rain or riv - ers flow, ____

do they know it's Christ - mas - time at ____ all?

Outro

Here's to you; raise a glass for ev - 'ry - one.

Here's to them un - der - neath that burn - ing sun. Do they know it's

Christ - mas - time at ____ all?   Feed the
(gain.)

Repeat and fade

world. _____   Let them know it's Christ - mas - time a -

Do You Hear What I Hear

Words and Music by Noel Regney and Gloria Shayne

D.S. al Coda

kite.   2., 3. Said   the   4. Said   the

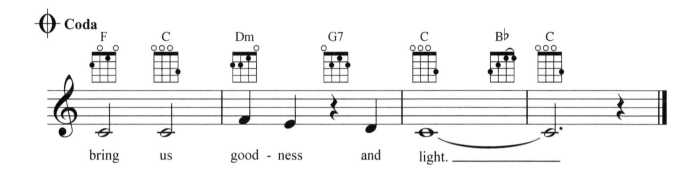

bring   us   good - ness   and   light. _____

Additional Lyrics

2. Said the little lamb to the shepherd boy:
   Do you hear what I hear?
   Ringing through the sky, shepherd boy,
   Do you hear what I hear?
   A song, a song, high above the tree,
   With a voice as big as the sea,
   With a voice as big as the sea.

3. Said the shepherd boy to the mighty king:
   Do you know what I know?
   In your palace warm, mighty king,
   Do you know what I know?
   A Child, a Child shivers in the cold;
   Let us bring Him silver and gold,
   Let us bring Him silver and gold.

4. Said the king to the people ev'rywhere:
   Listen to what I say!
   Pray for peace, people ev'rywhere.
   Listen to what I say!
   The Child, the Child, sleeping in the night,
   He will bring us goodness and light,
   He will bring us goodness and light.

Feliz Navidad

Music and Lyrics by José Feliciano

First note

Brightly

Chorus

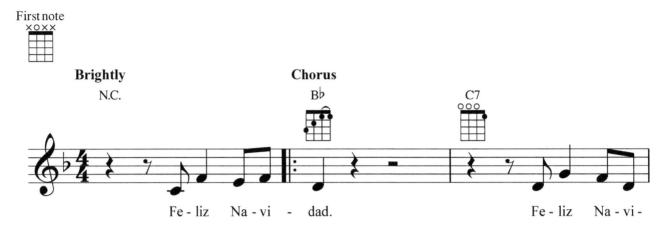

Fe - liz Na - vi - dad.   Fe - liz Na - vi -

dad.   Fe - liz Na - vi - dad. Pros - pe - ro a -

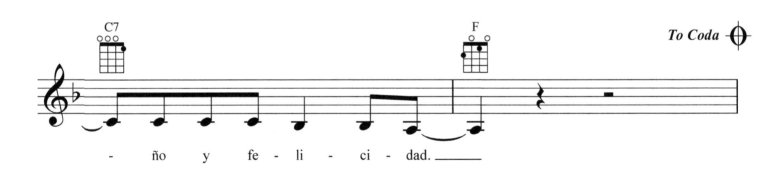

To Coda

- ño y fe - li - ci - dad. _____

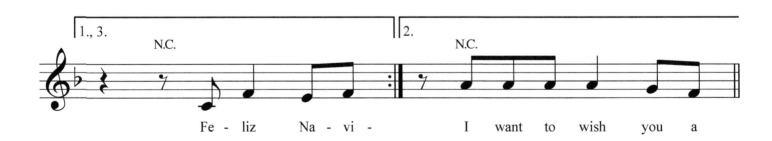

1., 3.

2.

Fe - liz Na - vi -   I want to wish you a

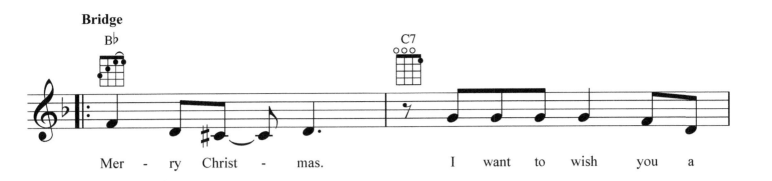

Mer - ry Christ - mas. I want to wish you a

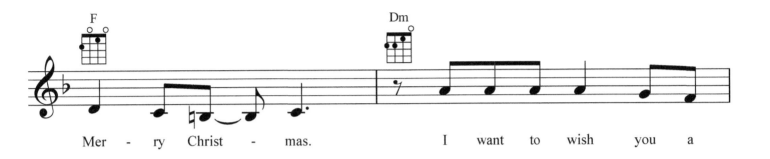

Mer - ry Christ - mas. I want to wish you a

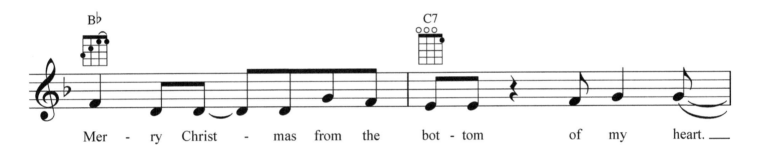

Mer - ry Christ - mas from the bot - tom of my heart. ___

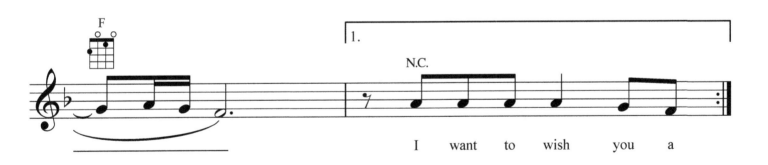

I want to wish you a

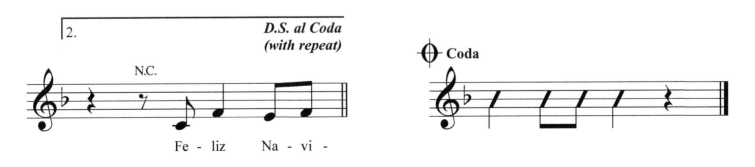

Fe - liz Na - vi -

Frosty the Snow Man

Words and Music by Steve Nelson and Jack Rollins

Verse

mag - ic in that old silk hat they found, for when they placed it
streets of town right to the traf - fic cop, and he on - ly paused a

on his head he be - gan to dance a - round. 2. Oh, Frost - y the
mo - ment when ___ he heard him hol - ler, "Stop!" 4. For Frost - y the

Snow Man was a - live as he could be, and the chil - dren say he could
Snow Man had to hur - ry on his way, but he waved good - bye say - in',

laugh and play just the same as you and me.
"Don't you cry, I'll be back a - gain some - day."

Outro

Thump - et - y thump thump, thump - et - y thump thump, look at Frost - y go.

Thump - et - y thump thump, thump - et - y thump thump, o - ver the hills of snow.

Happy Xmas
(War Is Over)
Written by John Lennon and Yoko Ono

Additional Lyrics

2. And so, this is Xmas for weak and for strong,
   The rich and the poor ones; the road is so long.
   And so, happy Xmas for black and for white,
   For the yellow and red ones; let's stop all the fights.

3. And so, this is Xmas, and what have we done?
   Another year over, a new one just begun.
   And so, happy Xmas; we hope you have fun,
   The near and the dear ones, the old and the young.

Have Yourself a Merry Little Christmas

from MEET ME IN ST. LOUIS
Words and Music by Hugh Martin and Ralph Blane

yore. Faith - ful friends who are dear to us gath - er

Outro-Verse

near to us once more. Through the years we

all will be to - geth - er, if the fates al -

low. Hang a shin - ing star up - on the high - est

bough, _____ and have your - self a

mer - ry lit - tle Christ - mas now. _____

Here Comes Santa Claus
(Right Down Santa Claus Lane)
Words and Music by Gene Autry and Oakley Haldeman

First note

night.
2. Here comes San - ta Claus! Here comes San - ta Claus!

night.
4. Here comes San - ta Claus! Here comes San - ta Claus!

Right down San - ta Claus Lane! He's got a bag that is

Right down San - ta Claus Lane! He'll come a - round when the

filled with toys for the boys and girls a - gain.

chimes ring out; then it's Christ - mas morn a - gain.

Hear those sleigh - bells jin - gle jan - gle; what a beau - ti - ful

Peace on earth will come to all if we just fol - low the

sight! Jump in bed, cov - er up your head, 'cause

light. Let's give thanks to the Lord a - bove, 'cause

1.
San - ta Claus comes to - night.

2.
San - ta Claus comes to - night.

A Holly Jolly Christmas

Music and Lyrics by Johnny Marks

Have a hol - ly jol - ly Christ - mas; it's the best time of the

year. I don't know if there'll be snow, but

have a cup of cheer. Have a hol - ly jol - ly

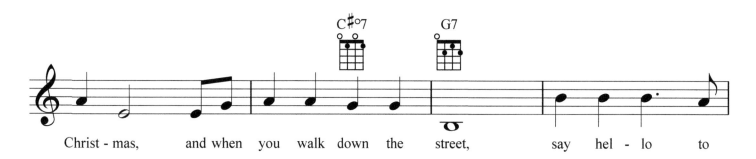

Christ - mas, and when you walk down the street, say hel - lo to

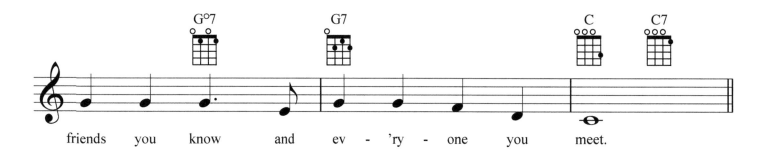

friends you know and ev - 'ry - one you meet.

I Heard the Bells on Christmas Day

Words by Henry Wadsworth Longfellow
Adapted by Johnny Marks
Music by Johnny Marks

Grandma Got Run Over by a Reindeer

Words and Music by Randy Brooks

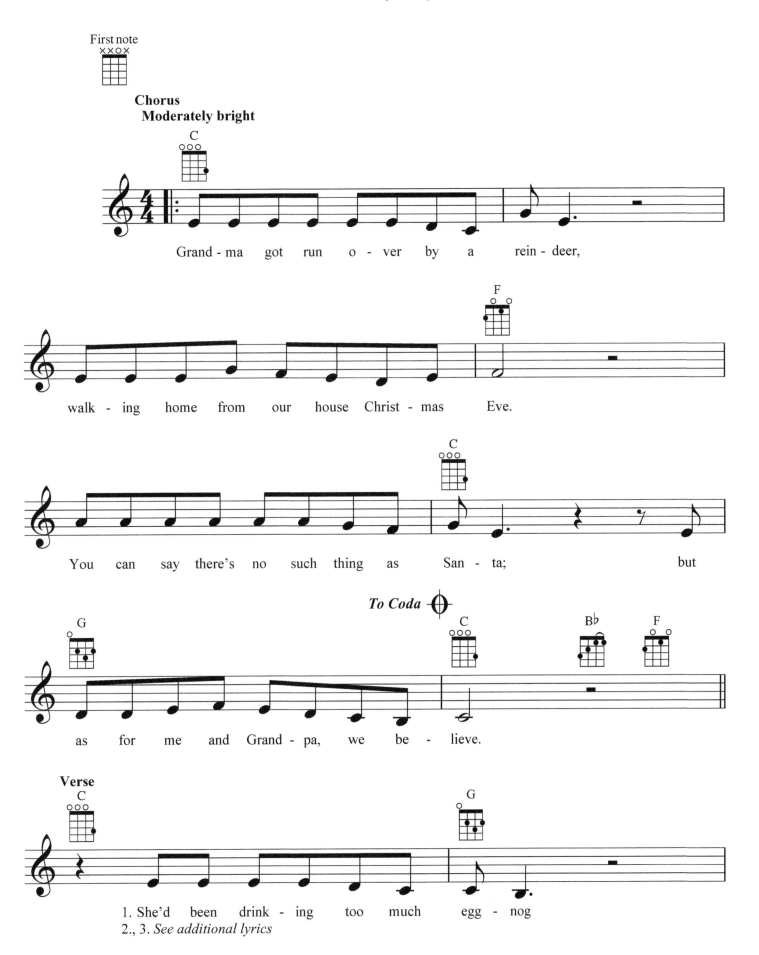

and we begged her not to go,

but she for - got her med - i - ca - tion and she

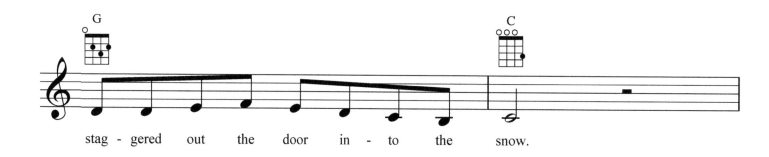

stag - gered out the door in - to the snow.

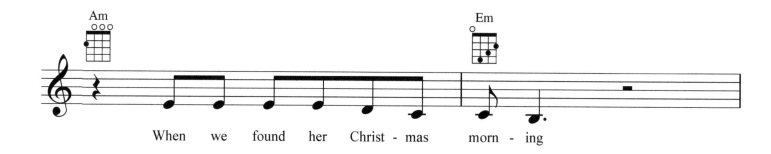

When we found her Christ - mas morn - ing

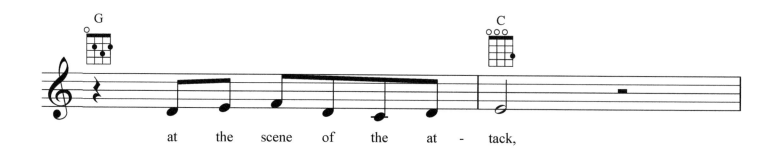

at the scene of the at - tack,

she had hoof - prints on her fore - head and in -

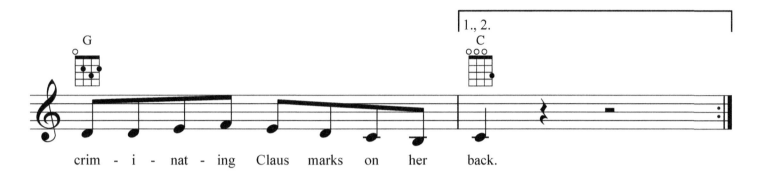

crim - i - nat - ing Claus marks on her back.

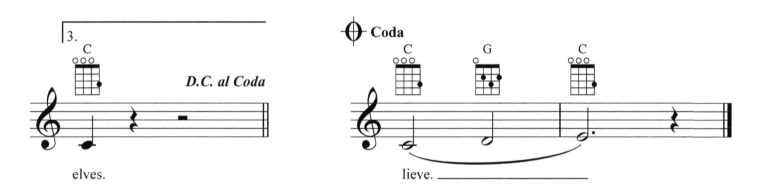

elves.

D.C. al Coda

Coda

lieve. _____

Additional Lyrics

2. Now we're all so proud of Grandpa;
   He's been taking this so well.
   See him in there watching football,
   Drinking beer and playing cards with Cousin Mel.
   It's not Christmas without Grandma;
   All the family's dressed in black.
   And we just can't help but wonder:
   Should we open up her gifts or send them back?

3. Now the goose is on the table,
   And the pudding made of fig,
   And the blue and silver candles
   That would just have matched the hair in Grandma's wig.
   I've warned all my friends and neighbors:
   Better watch out for yourselves.
   They should never give a license
   To a man who drives a sleigh and plays with elves.

I Wonder as I Wander

By John Jacob Niles

First note

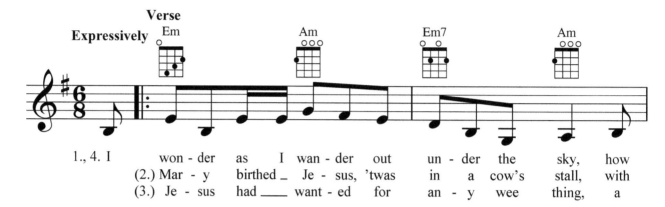

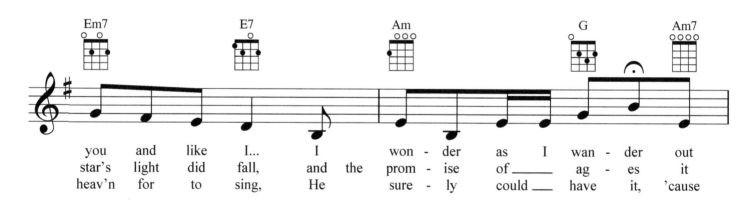

Merry Christmas, Baby

Words and Music by Lou Baxter and Johnny Moore

got good mu - sic on my ra - di - o. _____

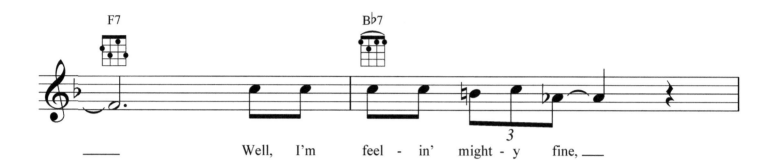

_____ Well, I'm feel - in' might - y fine, ___

got good mu - sic on my ra - di - o. _____ Well, I

want to kiss you, ba - by, while you're stand - in' 'neath the mis - tle - toe. _

Verse

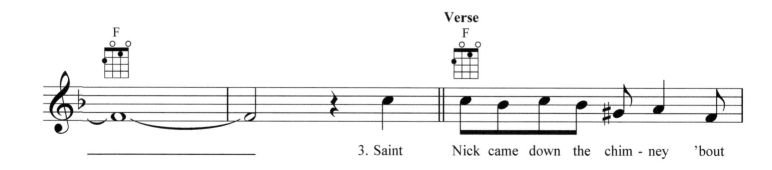

_____ 3. Saint Nick came down the chim - ney 'bout

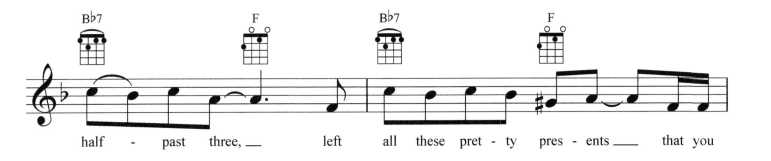

half - past three, ___ left all these pret - ty pres - ents ___ that you

see be - fore me. ___ Mer - ry Christ - mas, lit - tle ba - by.

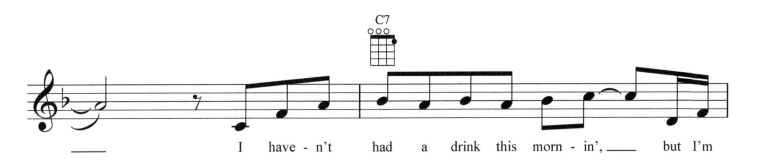

You sure ___ been good to me. ___

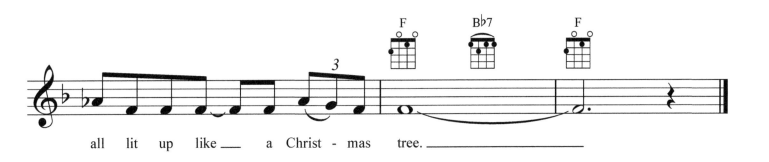

___ I have - n't had a drink this morn - in', ___ but I'm

all lit up like ___ a Christ - mas tree. ___

I'll Be Home for Christmas

Words and Music by Kim Gannon and Walter Kent

First note

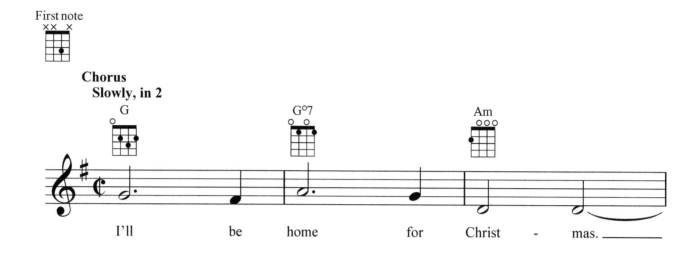

Chorus
Slowly, in 2

I'll be home for Christ - mas. ___

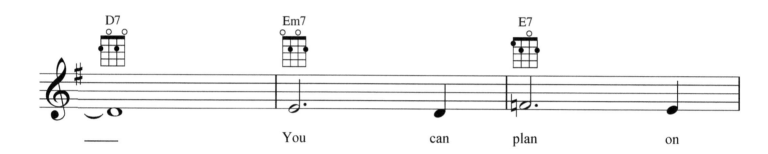

___ You can plan on

me. ___ Please have

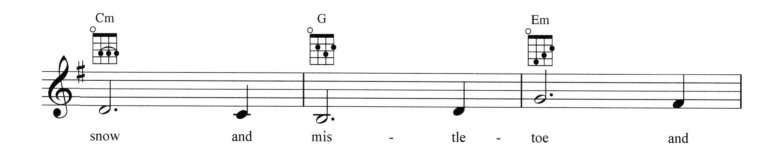

snow and mis - tle - toe and

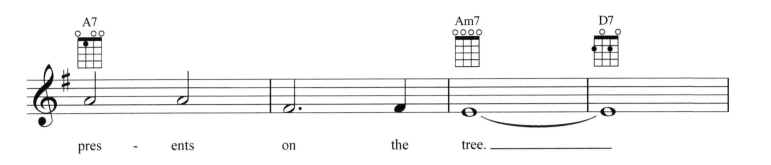

pres - ents on the tree. _____

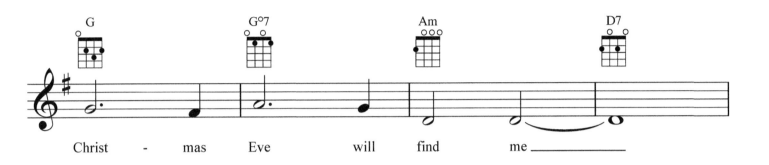

Christ - mas Eve will find me _____

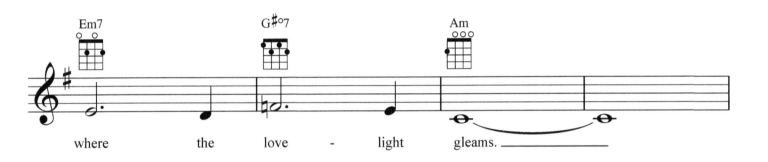

where the love - light gleams. _____

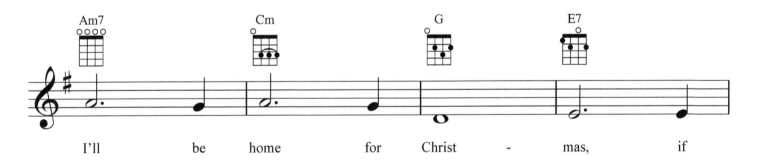

I'll be home for Christ - mas, if

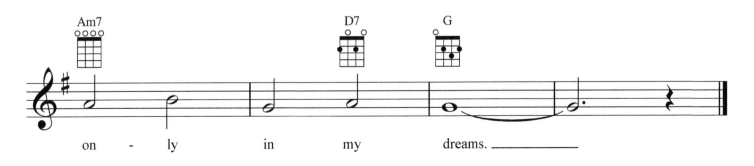

on - ly in my dreams. _____

It's Beginning to Look Like Christmas

By Meredith Willson

pret - ti - est sight to see   is   the   hol - ly   that   will   be   on   your
thing that will make them ring   is   the   car - ol   that   you   sing   right   with -

own   front   door.   A   pair   of
in   your

Bridge

hop - a - long boots and   a   pis - tol that shoots   is   the   wish   of   Bar - ney and Ben.

Dolls   that   will   talk   and   will   go   for   a   walk   is   the

hope   of   Jan - ice   and   Jen.   And   Mom   and   Dad   can   hard - ly   wait   for

D.S. al Coda

Coda

school   to   start   a - gain.   2. It's   be -   heart.

Jingle Bell Rock

Words and Music by Joe Beal and Jim Boothe

Last Christmas

Words and Music by George Michael

First note

Chorus
Slowly and freely

Last Christ - mas I gave you my heart, ___ but the

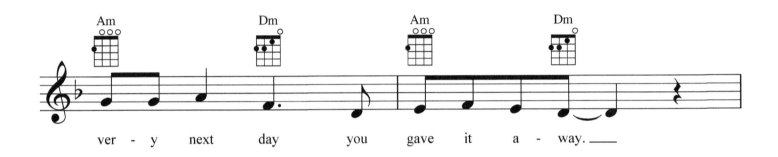

ver - y next day you gave it a - way. ___

This year, ___ to save me from tears, ___ I'll

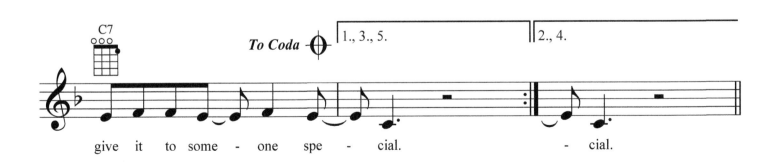

To Coda ⊕ | 1., 3., 5. | 2., 4.

give it to some - one spe - cial. - cial.

Interlude

(Instrumental)

Verse

1. Once bit - ten and
2. A crowd - ed room,

twice shy, _____ I keep my dis - tance but
friends with tired _____ eyes. __ I'm hid - ing from you

tears still catch __ my eye. _____ Tell me, ba - by,
and your soul __ of ice. _____ My God, I thought you were

do you rec - og - nize __ me? Well, it's been a year. __ It
some - one to re - ly __ on. Me, I guess I was a

does - n't   sur - prise ___   me.   Hap - py Christ - mas.   I
shoul - der   to   cry ___   on. A   face   on   a   lov - er with a

wrapped it   up   and sent it   with   a   note   say - ing, "I ___
fire   in   his   heart, _____   a   man un - der cov - er but you

___ love you." I   meant it. Now ___ I   know ___ what a fool ___
tore _____ me ___ a - part. _____

_____ I've been. __ But if you kissed   me   now, ___ I   know you'd
Ooh, _____ ooh, ___   now I've found a real ___ love. You'll nev - er

1.   2.   *D.C. al Coda*
                                                                                 (with repeat)

fool me   a - gain. ___   fool me   a - gain. ___

Verse
F

⊕ **Coda**

- cial.   3. A   face   on   a   lov - er with a

60

fire in his heart, ___ a man un - der cov - er but you

tore him a - part. ___ May - be next year I'll

give it to some - one, I'll give it to some - one spe -

Outro

- cial, spe - cial. ___ Some - one, ___

___ *(Instrumental)* some - one. I'll

Repeat ad lib. and fade

give it to some - one, I'll give it to some - one spe -

Let It Snow! Let It Snow! Let It Snow!

Words by Sammy Cahn
Music by Jule Styne

Bridge

snow! Let it snow! Let it snow! When we fi - nal - ly kiss good -

night, how I'll hate go - ing out in the storm! But if

you'll real - ly hold me tight, all the way home I'll be

Outro-Verse

warm. The fi - re is slow - ly dy - ing, and my

dear, we're still good - bye - ing. But as long as you love me

so, let it snow! Let it snow! Let it snow!

The Little Drummer Boy

Words and Music by Harry Simeone, Henry Onorati and Katherine Davis

First note

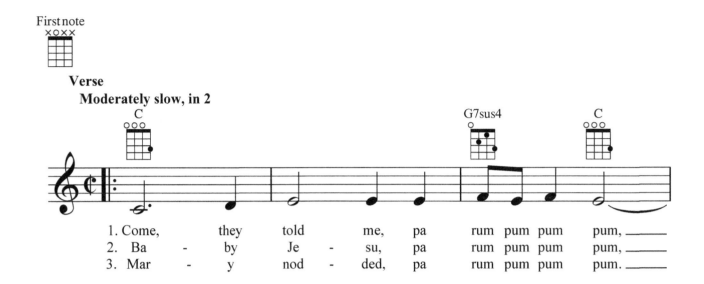

Verse
Moderately slow, in 2

1. Come, they told me, pa rum pum pum pum, _____
2. Ba - by Je - su, pa rum pum pum pum, _____
3. Mar - y nod - ded, pa rum pum pum pum. _____

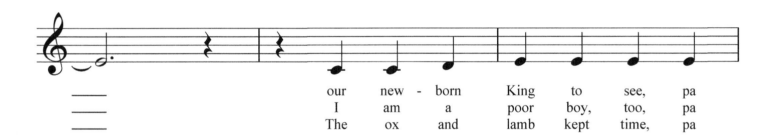

_____ our new - born King to see, pa
_____ I am a poor boy, too, pa
_____ The ox and lamb kept time, pa

rum pum pum pum. _____ Our fin - est
rum pum pum pum. _____ I have no
rum pum pum pum. _____ I played my

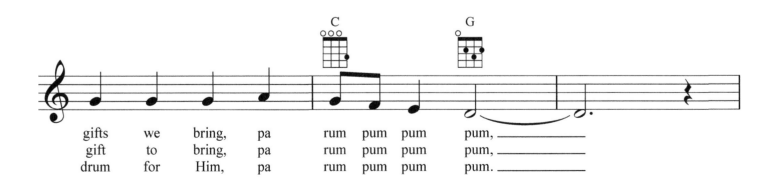

gifts we bring, pa rum pum pum pum, _____
gift to bring, pa rum pum pum pum, _____
drum for Him, pa rum pum pum pum. _____

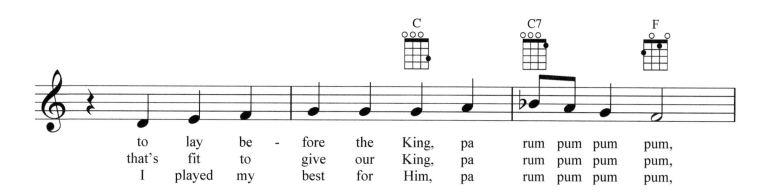

to lay be - fore the King, pa rum pum pum pum,
that's fit to give our King, pa rum pum pum pum,
I played my best for Him, pa rum pum pum pum,

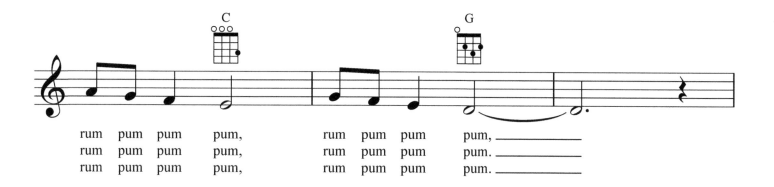

rum pum pum pum, rum pum pum pum, _____
rum pum pum pum, rum pum pum pum. _____
rum pum pum pum, rum pum pum pum. _____

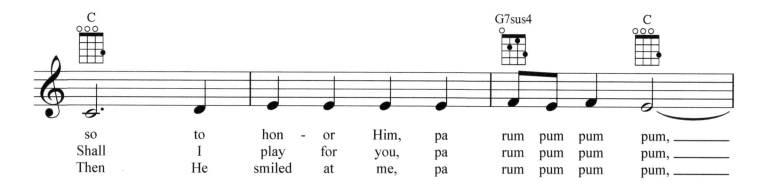

so to hon - or Him, pa rum pum pum pum, _____
Shall I play for you, pa rum pum pum pum, _____
Then He smiled at me, pa rum pum pum pum, _____

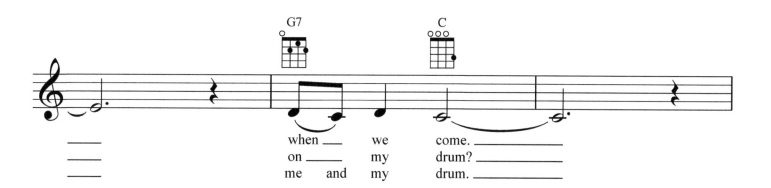

_____ when ___ we come. _____
_____ on _____ my drum? _____
_____ me and my drum. _____

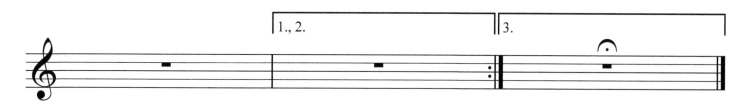

1., 2.   3.

A Marshmallow World

Words by Carl Sigman
Music by Peter De Rose

Mary, Did You Know?

Words and Music by Mark Lowry and Buddy Greene

soon de - liv - er you. _____ 2. Mar - y, did you

kissed the face __ of God? _ _____ Oh, Mar - y, did you

Interlude

know?

Mar - y, did you know?

Bridge

The blind will see, ___ the

deaf will hear, ___ the dead will live __ a - gain. ___ The lame will leap, ___ the

D.S. al Coda

dumb will speak __ the prais - es of ___ the Lamb. _____ 3. Mar - y, did you

Coda

- ing is the great I _____ AM?

The Most Wonderful Time of the Year

Words and Music by Eddie Pola and George Wyle

Nuttin' for Christmas

Words and Music by Roy C. Bennett and Sid Tepper

River

Words and Music by Joni Mitchell

First note

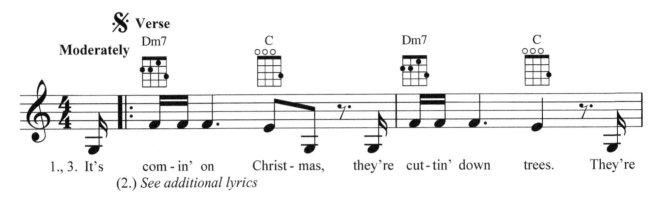

1., 3. It's com-in' on Christ-mas, they're cut-tin' down trees. They're

(2.) *See additional lyrics*

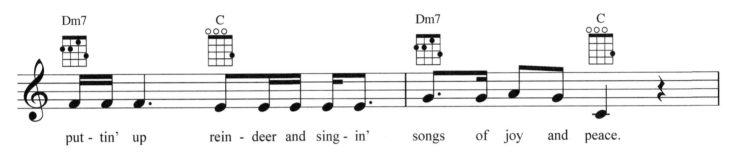

put-tin' up rein-deer and sing-in' songs of joy and peace.

Oh, I wish I ___ had a riv-er I could skate ___ a-

way ___ on.   But

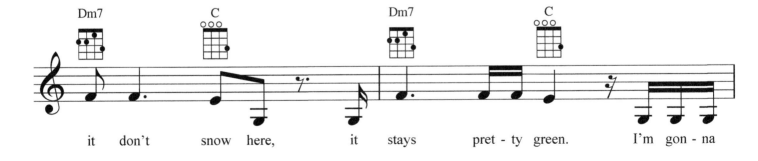

it don't snow here, it stays pret-ty green. I'm gon-na

Additional Lyrics

2. He tried hard to help me, you know, he put me at ease.
   He loved me so naughty, made me weak in the knees.
   Oh, I wish I had a river I could skate away on.
   I'm so hard to handle, I'm selfish and I'm sad.
   Now I've gone and lost the best baby that I ever had.
   Oh, I wish I had a river I could skate away on.

Please Come Home for Christmas

Words and Music by Charles Brown and Gene Redd

by New Year's night. _____ Friends and re-

Bridge

la - tions _____ send sal - u - ta - tions, _____

sure _____ as the stars shine a - bove. _____ For this is

Christ - mas, _____ yes, Christ - mas, my dear. _____

_____ It's the time of year _____ to be with the one _____ you

Outro-Verse

love. So, won't you tell me _____ you'll nev - er - more

Additional Lyrics

2. Choirs will be singing "Silent Night,"
   Christmas carols by candlelight.
   Please come home for Christmas,
   Please come home for Christmas.
   If not for Christmas, by New Year's night.

Rudolph the Red-Nosed Reindeer

Music and Lyrics by Johnny Marks

Ru-dolph the red - nosed rein - deer had a ver - y shin - y

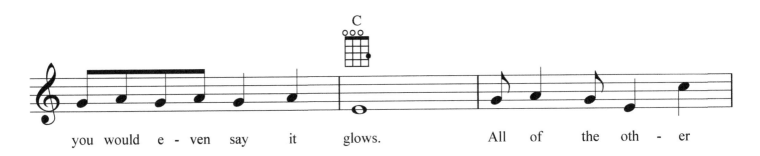

nose, and if you ev - er saw it, you would e - ven say it glows. All of the oth - er

rein - deer used to laugh and call him names; they nev - er let poor Ru - dolph join in an - y rein - deer

Run Rudolph Run

Music and Lyrics by Johnny Marks and Marvin Brodie

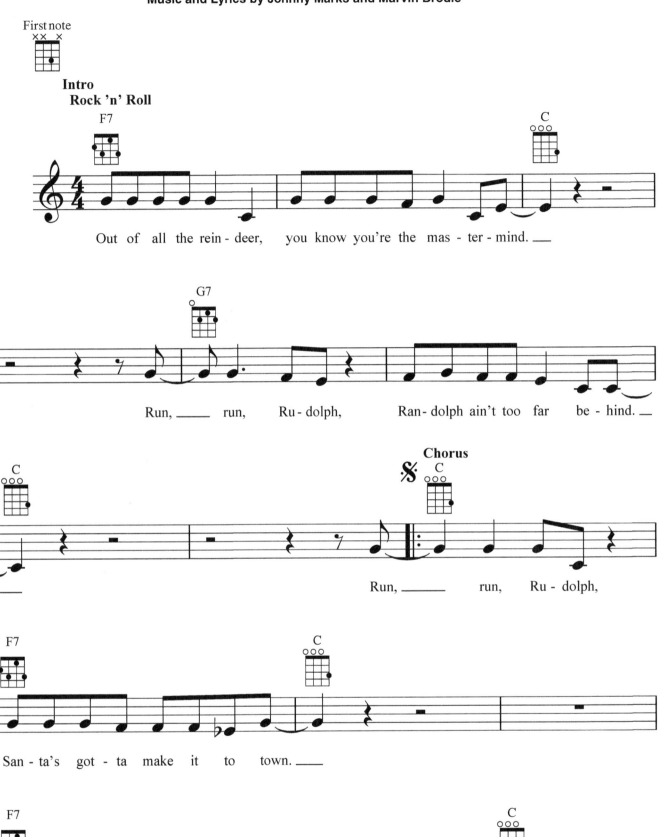

Santa Baby

By Joan Javits, Phil Springer and Tony Springer

First note

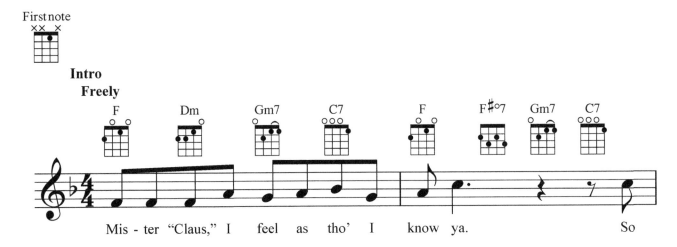

Intro
Freely

Mis - ter "Claus," I feel as tho' I know ya. So

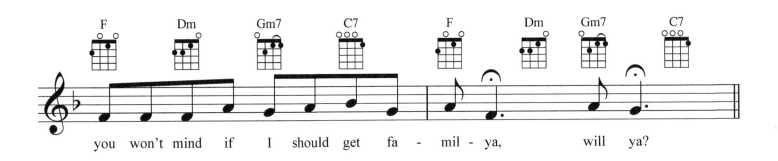

you won't mind if I should get fa - mil - ya, will ya?

Verse
Moderately, relaxed

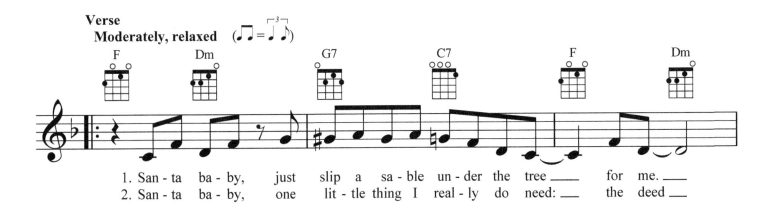

1. San - ta ba - by, just slip a sa - ble un - der the tree _____ for me. _____
2. San - ta ba - by, one lit - tle thing I real - ly do need: _____ the deed _____

Been an aw - ful good girl, _____ San - ta ba - by, so
to a plat - i - num mine, _____ San - ta hon - ey, so

have - n't kissed. ___ Next year I could be
Tif - fa - ny. ____ I real - ly do be -

just as good ___ if you check off my Christ - mas list.
lieve in you; ___ let's see if you be - lieve in me.

Outro-Verse

San - ta ba - by, I want a yacht and real - ly that's not ___
San - ta ba - by, for - got to men - tion one lit - tle thing: ___

___ a lot. ___ Been an an - gel all year, ___
___ a ring! ___ I don't mean on the phone, ___

___ San - ta ba - by, so hur - ry down the chim - ney to - night.
___ San - ta ba - by, so hur - ry down the chim - ney to - night. ___

Sleigh Ride

Music by Leroy Anderson
Words by Mitchell Parish

First note

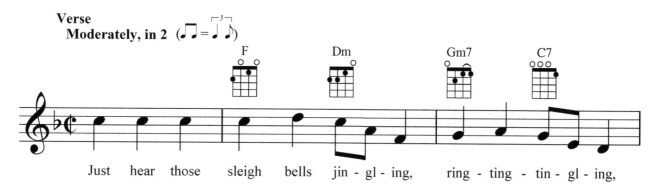

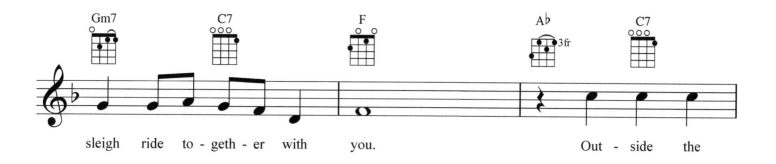

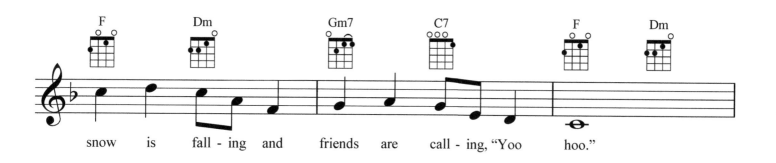

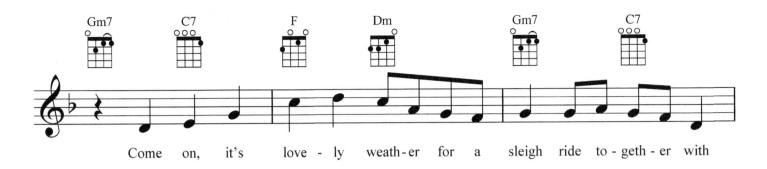

Come on, it's love-ly weath-er for a sleigh ride to-geth-er with

Bridge

you. _____ Gid-dy - yap, gid-dy-yap, gid-dy-

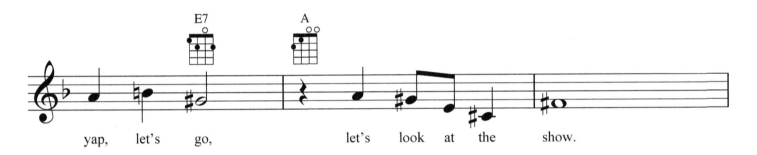

yap, let's go, let's look at the show.

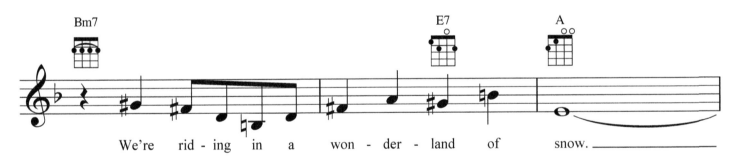

We're rid-ing in a won-der-land of snow. _____

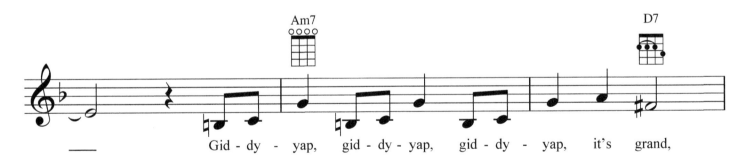

_____ Gid-dy - yap, gid-dy-yap, gid-dy-yap, it's grand,

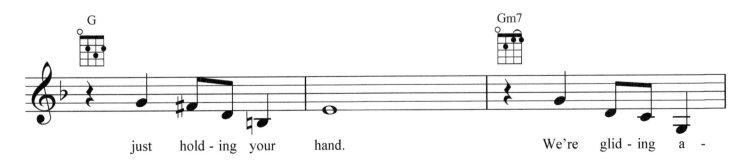

just hold-ing your hand. We're glid-ing a-

long with a song of a win-ter-y fair-y- land. Our cheeks are

Outro-Verse

nice and ros - y, and com - fy co - zy are we.

We're snug - gled up to - geth - er like two birds of a feath - er would

be. Let's take that road be - fore us and

sing a cho - rus or two. Come on, it's

love - ly weath-er for a sleigh ride to-geth-er with you. _____

Santa Claus Is Comin' to Town

Words by Haven Gillespie
Music by J. Fred Coots

Bridge

He sees you when you're sleep - ing, he knows when you're a -

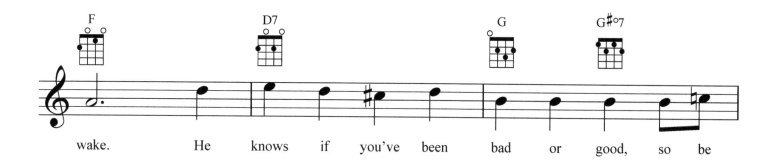

wake. He knows if you've been bad or good, so be

Outro-Verse

good for good - ness sake! Oh, you bet - ter watch out, you

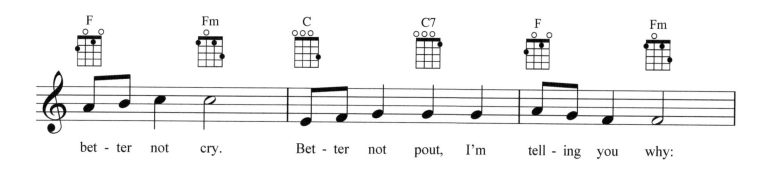

bet - ter not cry. Bet - ter not pout, I'm tell - ing you why:

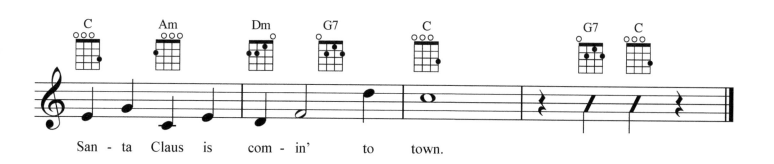

San - ta Claus is com - in' to town.

Silver and Gold

Music and Lyrics by Johnny Marks

First note

Chorus
Slowly and expressively

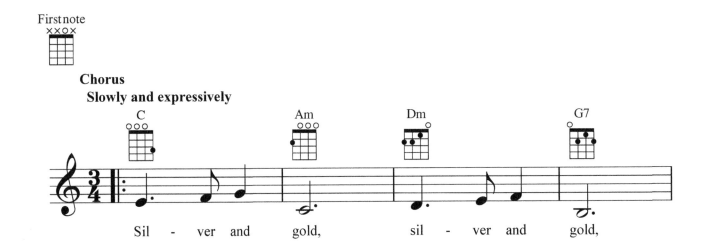

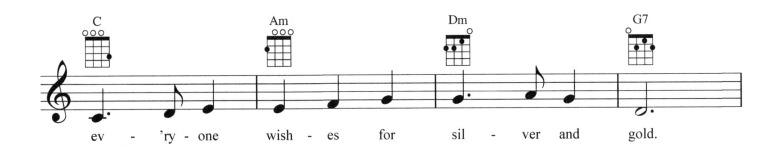

Sil - ver and gold, sil - ver and gold,

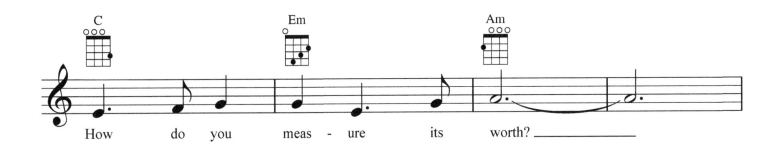

ev - 'ry - one wish - es for sil - ver and gold.

How do you meas - ure its worth? _____

Just by the pleas - ure it gives here on earth.

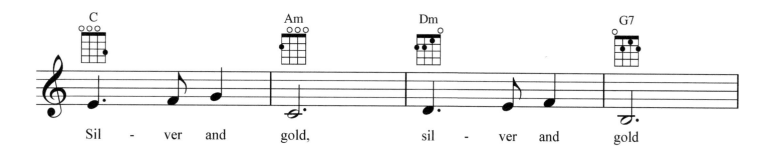

Sil - ver and gold, sil - ver and gold

mean so much more when I see _____

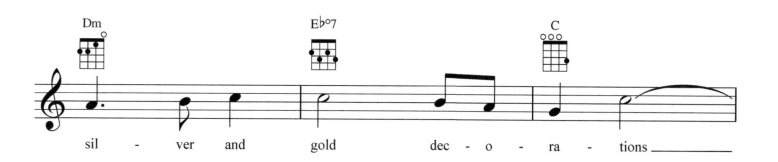

sil - ver and gold dec - o - ra - tions _____

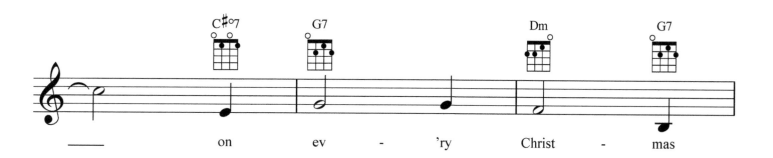

_____ on ev - 'ry Christ - mas

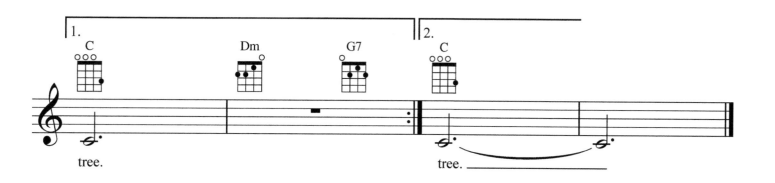

1.   tree.   2.   tree. _____

Silver Bells

from the Paramount Picture THE LEMON DROP KID
Words and Music by Jay Livingston and Ray Evans

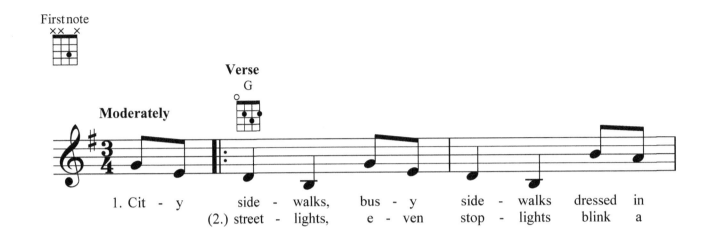

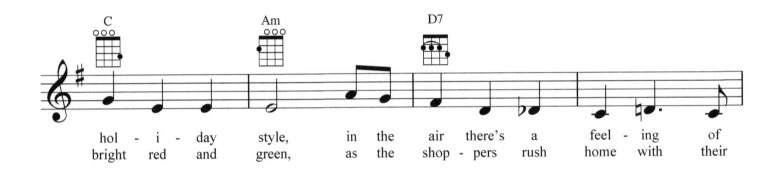

1. Cit - y side - walks, bus - y side - walks dressed in
(2.) street - lights, e - ven stop - lights blink a

hol - i - day style, in the air there's a feel - ing of
bright red and green, as the shop - pers rush home with their

Christ - mas.
treas - ures.

Chil - dren laugh - ing, peo - ple pass - ing, meet - ing
Hear the snow crunch, see the kids bunch, this is

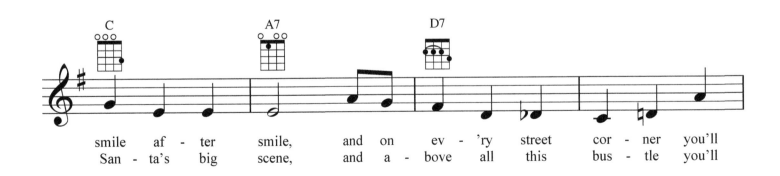

smile af - ter smile, and on ev - 'ry street cor - ner you'll
San - ta's big scene, and a - bove all this bus - tle you'll

Chorus

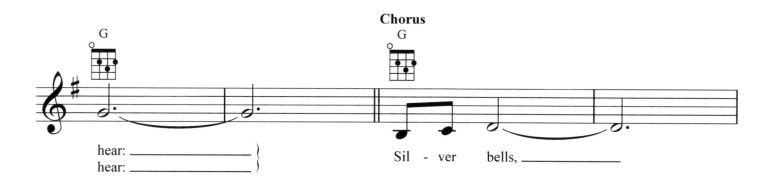

hear: _____
hear: _____ }
Sil - ver bells, _____

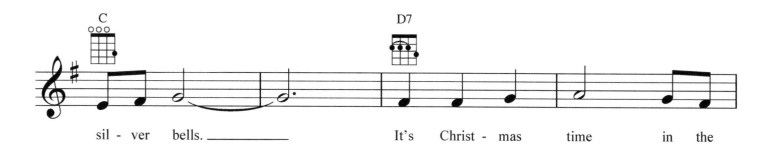

sil - ver bells. _____ It's Christ - mas time in the

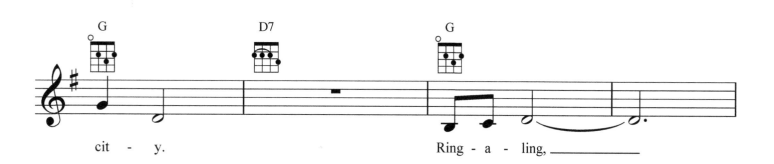

cit - y. Ring - a - ling, _____

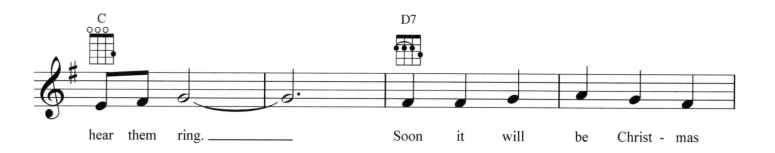

hear them ring. _____ Soon it will be Christ - mas

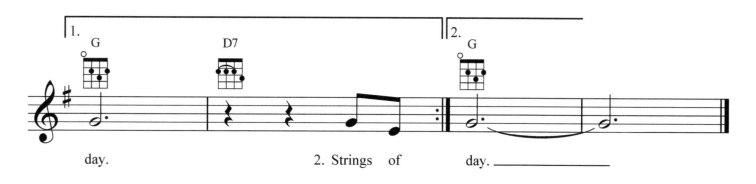

day. 2. Strings of day. _____

This Christmas

Words and Music by Donny Hathaway and Nadine McKinnor

Christ - mas _____ for _ me. _____ (Instrumental)

1., 2.

3.   **Outro**

Mer - ry Christ - mas. _____ (Instrumental)

Shake your hand, shake your hand now. (Instrumental)

Wish your broth - er mer - ry Christ - mas _____ (Instrumental)

all o - ver the land _____ now. (Instrumental)

We Need a Little Christmas

from MAME

Music and Lyric by Jerry Herman

First note

Verse
Brightly, in 2

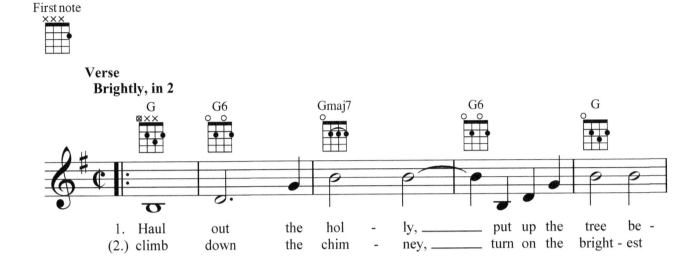

1. Haul out the hol - ly, _____ put up the tree be -
(2.) climb down the chim - ney, _____ turn on the bright - est

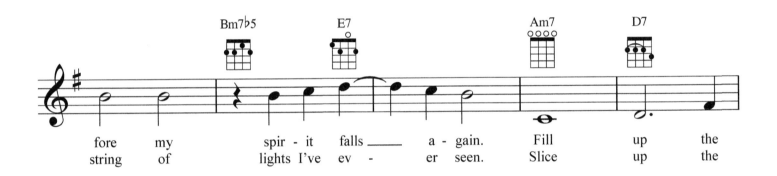

fore my spir - it falls _____ a - gain. Fill up the
string of lights I've ev - er seen. Slice up the

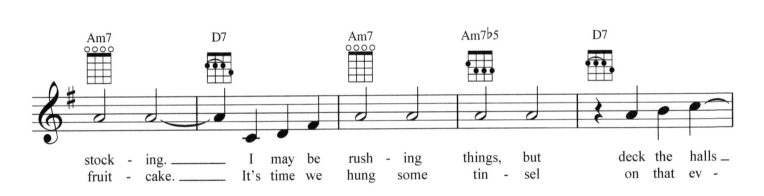

stock - ing. _____ I may be rush - ing things, but deck the halls _____
fruit - cake. _____ It's time we hung some tin - sel on that ev -

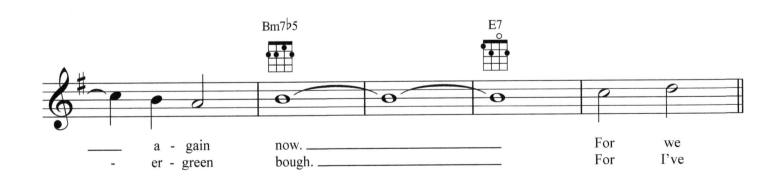

_____ a - gain now. _____ For we
- er - green bough. _____ For I've

What Are You Doing New Year's Eve?

By Frank Loesser

1. May - be it's much too ear - ly in the game, __
2. Won - der whose arms will hold you good and tight __

ah, but I thought I'd ask you just the same: __
when it's ex - act - ly twelve o' - clock that night, __

What are you do - ing New Year's, New Year's
wel - com - ing in the new year,

Eve?

New Year's Eve.

Bridge

May - be I'm cra - zy to sup - pose

Outro-Verse

I'd ev - er be the one you chose

out of the thou - sand in - vi - ta - tions

you'll re - ceive. Ah, but in case I

stand one lit - tle chance, ___ here comes the jack - pot

ques - tion in ad - vance: ___ What are you do - ing

New Year's, New Year's Eve?

White Christmas

from the Motion Picture Irving Berlin's HOLIDAY INN
Words and Music by Irving Berlin

Winter Wonderland

Words by Dick Smith
Music by Felix Bernard

Firstnote

Verse
Moderately bright

C   G7

1., 3. Sleigh-bells ring, are you lis-t'nin'? In the lane, snow is

glis-t'nin'. A beau-ti-ful sight, __ we're hap-py to-night, __

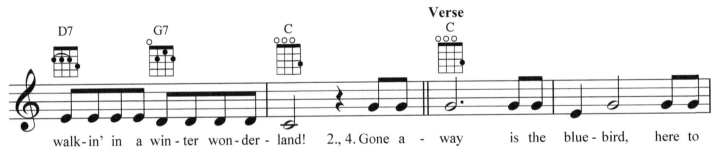

D7   G7   C   Verse C

walk-in' in a win-ter won-der-land! 2., 4. Gone a-way is the blue-bird, here to

G7

stay is a new bird. { He sings a love song __ } as
{ He's sing-ing a song __ }

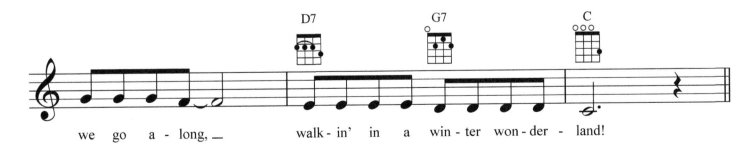

D7   G7   C

we go a-long, __ walk-in' in a win-ter won-der-land!

Bridge

In the mead-ow we can build a snow - man, { then pre-tend that he is Par - son
  and pre-tend that he's a cir - cus

Brown. He'll say, "Are you mar - ried?" We'll say, "No, man! But
clown. We'll have lots of fun with Mis - ter Snow - man, un -

you can do the job when you're in town!" Lat - er
til the oth - er kid - dies knock him down! When it

Outro-Verse

on, we'll con - spi - re as we dream by the
snows, ain't it thrill - in', tho' your nose gets a

fi - re, to face un - a - fraid __ the plans that we made, __ }
chill - in'? We'll frol - ic and play __ the Es - ki - mo way, __ }

1.
walk - in' in a win - ter won - der - land!

3. Sleigh-bells

2.
land!

Wonderful Christmastime

Words and Music by Paul McCartney

choir of chil - dren sing their song. (They

To Coda

prac - ticed all year long.) Ding

Chorus

dong, ding dong, ding dong. We're sim - ply

hav - ing a won - der - ful Christ - mas - time. Sim - ply

D.C. al Coda (take 2nd ending)

hav - ing a won - der - ful Christ - mas - time.

Coda

Ding dong, ding dong, ding dong, ding

Additional Lyrics

2. The party's on, the feelin's here
   That only comes this time of year.

3. The word is out about the town,
   To lift a glass. Oh, don't look down.

Somewhere in My Memory

from the Twentieth Century Fox Motion Picture HOME ALONE
Words by Leslie Bricusse
Music by John Williams

You're All I Want for Christmas

Words and Music by Glen Moore and Seger Ellis

First note

Verse
Freely, in 2

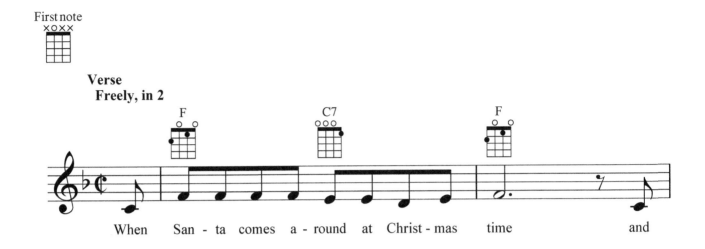

When San - ta comes a - round at Christ - mas time and

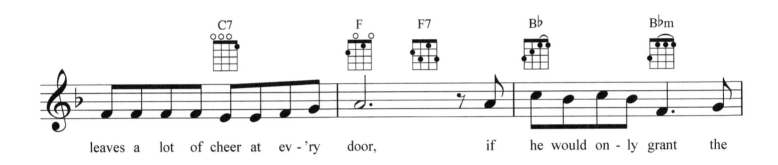

leaves a lot of cheer at ev - 'ry door, if he would on - ly grant the

wish in my heart, I would nev - er ask for more. You're

Chorus
Moderately

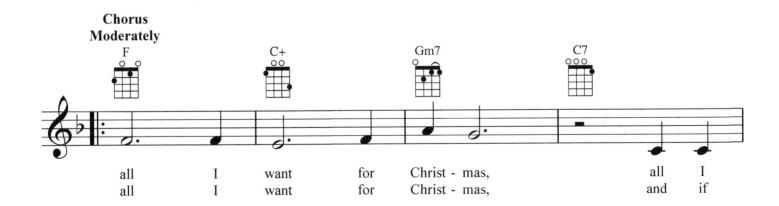

all I want for Christ - mas, all I
all I want for Christ - mas, and if

want my whole life through. _____ Each
all my dreams come true, _____ then

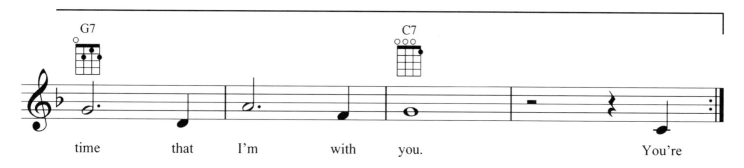

1.
day is just like Christ - mas _____ an - y
I'll a -

time that I'm with you. You're

2.
wake on Christ - mas morn - ing and find

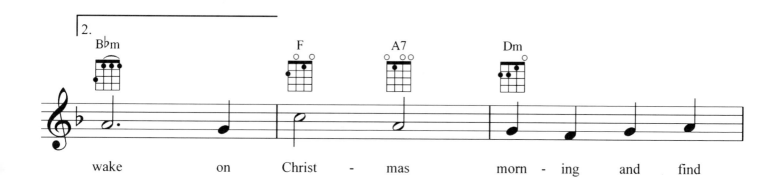

my stock - ing filled with you. _____

UKULELE CHORD SONGBOOKS

This series features convenient 6" x 9" books with complete lyrics and chord symbols for dozens of great songs. Each song also includes chord grids at the top of every page and the first notes of the melody for easy reference.

ACOUSTIC ROCK

60 tunes: American Pie • Band on the Run • Catch the Wind • Daydream • Every Rose Has Its Thorn • Hallelujah • Iris • More Than Words • Patience • The Sound of Silence • Space Oddity • Sweet Talkin' Woman • Wake up Little Susie • Who'll Stop the Rain • and more.
00702482 . . . . $15.99

THE BEATLES

100 favorites: Across the Universe • Carry That Weight • Dear Prudence • Good Day Sunshine • Here Comes the Sun • If I Fell • Love Me Do • Michelle • Ob-La-Di, Ob-La-Da • Revolution • Something • Ticket to Ride • We Can Work It Out • and many more.
00703065 . . . . $19.99

BEST SONGS EVER

70 songs: All I Ask of You • Bewitched • Edelweiss • Just the Way You Are • Let It Be • Memory • Moon River • Over the Rainbow • Someone to Watch over Me • Unchained Melody • You Are the Sunshine of My Life • You Raise Me Up • and more.
00117050 . . . . $16.99

CHILDREN'S SONGS

80 classics: Alphabet Song • "C" Is for Cookie • Do-Re-Mi • I'm Popeye the Sailor Man • Mickey Mouse March • Oh! Susanna • Polly Wolly Doodle • Puff the Magic Dragon • The Rainbow Connection • Sing • Three Little Fishies (Itty Bitty Poo) • and many more.
00702473 . . . . $14.99

CHRISTMAS CAROLS

75 favorites: Away in a Manger • Coventry Carol • The First Noel • Good King Wenceslas • Hark! the Herald Angels Sing • I Saw Three Ships • Joy to the World • O Little Town of Bethlehem • Still, Still, Still • Up on the Housetop • What Child Is This? • and more.
00702474 . . . . $14.99

CHRISTMAS SONGS

55 Christmas classics: Do They Know It's Christmas? • Frosty the Snow Man • Happy Xmas (War Is Over) • Jingle-Bell Rock • Little Saint Nick • The Most Wonderful Time of the Year • White Christmas • and more.
00101776 . . . . $14.99

ISLAND SONGS

60 beach party tunes: Blue Hawaii • Day-O (The Banana Boat Song) • Don't Worry, Be Happy • Island Girl • Kokomo • Lovely Hula Girl • Mele Kalikimaka • Red, Red Wine • Surfer Girl • Tiny Bubbles • Ukulele Lady • and many more.
00702471 . . . . $16.99

150 OF THE MOST BEAUTIFUL SONGS EVER

150 melodies: Always • Bewitched • Candle in the Wind • Endless Love • In the Still of the Night • Just the Way You Are • Memory • The Nearness of You • People • The Rainbow Connection • Smile • Unchained Melody • What a Wonderful World • Yesterday • and more.
00117051 . . . . $24.99

PETER, PAUL & MARY

Over 40 songs: And When I Die • Blowin' in the Wind • Goodnight, Irene • If I Had a Hammer (The Hammer Song) • Leaving on a Jet Plane • Puff the Magic Dragon • This Land Is Your Land • We Shall Overcome • Where Have All the Flowers Gone? • and more.
00121822 . . . . $12.99

THREE CHORD SONGS

60 songs: Bad Case of Loving You • Bang a Gong (Get It On) • Blue Suede Shoes • Cecilia • Get Back • Hound Dog • Kiss • Me and Bobby McGee • Not Fade Away • Rock This Town • Sweet Home Chicago • Twist and Shout • You Are My Sunshine • and more.
00702483 . . . . $14.99

TOP HITS

31 hits: The A Team • Born This Way • Forget You • Ho Hey • Jar of Hearts • Little Talks • Need You Now • Rolling in the Deep • Teenage Dream • Titanium • We Are Never Ever Getting Back Together • and more.
00115929 . . . . $14.99

Prices, contents, and availability subject to change without notice.

www.halleonard.com